Brittany
Travel Guide

Quick Trips Series

No part of this publication may be reproduced, stored in a retrieval system, or transmitted, in any form or by any means without the prior written permission of the publisher, nor be otherwise circulated in any form of binding or cover other than that in which it is published and without similar condition being imposed on the subsequent purchaser. If there are any errors or omissions in copyright acknowledgements the publisher will be pleased to insert the appropriate acknowledgement in any subsequent printing of this publication. Although we have taken all reasonable care in researching this book we make no warranty about the accuracy or completeness of its content and disclaim all liability arising from its use.

Copyright © 2016, Astute Press
All Rights Reserved.

Table of Contents

BRITTANY — 6
- 🌍 CUSTOMS & CULTURE 7
- 🌍 GEOGRAPHY 8
- 🌍 WEATHER & BEST TIME TO VISIT 10

SIGHTS & ACTIVITIES: WHAT TO SEE & DO — 11
- 🌍 RENNES 11
- 🌍 FOUGÈRES & VITRÉ 13
  - Château de Fougères 13
  - Château de Vitré 14
  - Château des Rochers-Sévigné 14
- 🌍 JOSSELIN 16
  - Chateau de Josselin 16
  - Kerguéhennec Sculpture Garden 16
- 🌍 DINAN 18
  - Musée du Château (Castle Museum) 18
- 🌍 SAINT-MALO 19
  - Château de St-Malo 19
  - Grand Aquarium 19
- 🌍 DINARD 22
  - Casino Barrière de Dinard 22
  - Dinard Golf Club 22
- 🌍 PINK GRANITE COAST (CÔTE DU GRANIT ROSE) 23
  - Glass Studios of Bréhat 23
- 🌍 MORLAIX & ROSCOFF 25

    Queen Anne's House 25
    Château de Suscinio 26
🌐 **BREST** 29
    Oceanopolis 29
    Ecomusée d'Ouessant 29
🌐 **DOUARNENEZ & LOCRONAN** 32
🌐 **QUIMPER** 34
🌐 **AURAY, CARNAC & QUIBERON** 36
🌐 **VANNES** 37

BUDGET TIPS   38

🌐 **ACCOMMODATION** 38
    Rennes 38
    St. Malo 39
    Brest 40
    Quimper 41
    Vannes 42
🌐 **RESTAURANTS, CAFÉS & BARS** 43
    Dinard 43
    Vitré 44
    Auray 44
    Quiberon 45
    Douarnenez 46
🌐 **SHOPPING** 47
    Quimper 47
    Roscoff 48
    Rennes 49
    Cancale 49

KNOW BEFORE YOU GO   52

🌐 **ENTRY REQUIREMENTS** 52
🌐 **HEALTH INSURANCE** 53

- 🌐 **Travelling with Pets** 53
- 🌐 **Airports** 54
- 🌐 **Airlines** 56
- 🌐 **Currency** 57
- 🌐 **Banking & ATMs** 57
- 🌐 **Credit Cards** 57
- 🌐 **Tourist Taxes** 58
- 🌐 **Reclaiming VAT** 58
- 🌐 **Tipping Policy** 59
- 🌐 **Mobile Phones** 59
- 🌐 **Dialling Code** 60
- 🌐 **Emergency Numbers** 60
- 🌐 **Time Zone** 61
- 🌐 **Daylight Savings Time** 62
- 🌐 **School Holidays** 62
- 🌐 **Driving Laws** 62
- 🌐 **Drinking Laws** 63
- 🌐 **Smoking Laws** 64
- 🌐 **Electricity** 64
- 🌐 **Food & Drink** 65

BRITTANY TRAVEL GUIDE

Brittany

Brittany (*Bretagne* in French) in France's northwest region was first known to the Romans as Lesser Britain. The famous peninsula is located close to Normandy and the Loire Valley of France.

A stay in Brittany will leave you feeling like you're in a perpetual Celtic fairytale with many of its towns and cities having retained their medieval architecture.

Its dramatic windswept coastline changes with the weather from hauntingly, beautifully melancholy to utterly sublime – made all the more mysterious when you learn about the regions swashbuckling pirate past.

BRITTANY TRAVEL GUIDE

Its forests figure prominently in Arthurian legend. Even if you don't have an overactive imagination, you'll no doubt feel the magic or – at the very least – the charm of this land.

For those seeking a more urban excursion, Brittany has several large cities with the kind of nightlife and entertainment that are sure to please. A few nights out in Rennes (Brittany's capital) or Brest are sure to satisfy your night owl cravings.

But in general, be prepared to relax and move at a slower pace here; this isn't Paris. There's no need to worry about looking *trés chic*. Rather, be sure to pack a bathing suit and some good walking shoes, because you're going to see some stunning sights, eat some wonderful food and get to know some incredibly welcoming people.

🌍 Customs & Culture

Brittany is French but culturally unique unto itself. During the 5th century as the Anglo-Saxons pushed into Great Britain, many of the Celtic people, particularly those from Cornwall, left and resettled themselves in Brittany. Bretons (as the people here are called) are cousins to the Cornish, Welsh, Scots and Irish.

So is the Breton language, which, remarkably, has not died out. In fact, an increasing number of the population is bilingual (but your high school French will still be put to good use since that is the dominant language – and most people also speak English). Still, it couldn't hurt you to pick up a Breton phrasebook and learn a few words – you'll be sure to impress some folks.

BRITTANY TRAVEL GUIDE

Municipally speaking, Brittany is an administrative region that is broken into four departments: Ile-et-Vilaine, which includes the region's capital, Rennes, and seaside St-Malo; Côtes D'Armor, which includes the Emerald Coast and the Pink Granite Coast; Finistière, where you'll find Brest and Quimper; and Morbihan, which encompasses Vannes.

🌍 Geography

The Breton peninsula stretches into the Atlantic, making it the westernmost part of metropolitan France (not including France's many overseas territories). It is directly south of Cornwall, UK.

There are several ways to get to Brittany. If you're coming from the UK or Ireland, you can take ferries from Plymouth, Poole, Portsmouth, Weymouth, Cork and

BRITTANY TRAVEL GUIDE

Rosslare to either Roscoff or St-Malo. It's an affordable way to travel, just be sure that you have time to dedicate an entire day to travel as the trip takes 5-9 hours, depending upon where you board and disembark.

If you opt to fly, you can do so directly to Rennes, Dinard, Brest or Quimper if you're flying from the UK, Ireland or other points in Europe. If you're coming from further afield you will likely have to make a connection in Paris. At that point, you might want to consider switching to a train to save a little cash (compared to taking a connecting flight).

A high speed (TGV) train will take you from Paris to Rennes in two hours, to St.-Malo in three, and to Brest or Quimper in four. Once in Brittany, you can continue to travel by train, but it might be wiser to rent a car to allow you to explore places that are off the tourist path.

🌍 Weather & Best Time to Visit

Keep in mind that Brittany is a fairly large region and at least seventy percent of its regional border is coastline. This has an effect on the climate both for the good (it enjoys a warmer maritime climate) and the bad (it rains a lot). The good is that it has a warm maritime climate similar to Cornwall; the bad is that it rains a lot – but often not for very long, and there are many sunny, cloudless days as well. (Still, be sure to pack your rain gear.)

Generally speaking, summer temperatures can reach as high as 30 °C (92 °F), especially inland. Proximity to the sea will cause variations in temperature, however. Winter temperatures are mild and rarely drop to freezing.

Summer temperatures are not unbearable, particularly by the sea, but even if you're inland Brittany's cities and towns aren't as hot as, say, Paris, where one is surrounded by stone, concrete and tarmac on all sides.

Sights & Activities: What to See & Do

🌍 Rennes

Rennes is the capital of Brittany and has the largest population of any Breton city. Since 60,000 of its 200,000 residents are students, Rennes is known for having a captivating nightlife – a perfect place to start (or end) your holiday in Brittany with a night on the town before heading off to the smaller, quainter seaside towns.

With that in mind, you'll want to check out Rue Saint Michel, which locals refer to as *la rue de la soif* ("Street of Thirst"). This street is lined *only* by bars and cafes on both sides. Thursday nights (the night before students leave for home) are particularly raucous, which is either a recommendation or a warning depending on what you're looking for.

During the day you'll want to take some time to relax in Thabor Gardens (*Park du Thabor*). This park occupies almost 25 acres in the city center and is a stunning example of 19th century French garden design. It's a perfect place to sit with an espresso and a book (and perhaps recover from the night before).

Art lovers won't want to miss Rennes' Art Museum (*Musée des Beaux Arts*) which houses a collection of art from the 14th century to the present, including many works by Breton artists.

BRITTANY TRAVEL GUIDE

In 1720, Rennes was devastated by a fire that lasted six days. Very little of the city's medieval architecture survived, allowing for modern neo-classical buildings and a grid-like street plan to grow from the embers.

Walking the Place des Lices, you'll discover some of the medieval half-timbered buildings that did survive, as well as the bustling market that exists there today. Buy some artisanal nougat to snack on while you walk, and if you happen to spot the Cathedral down the lane, head in that direction.

Construction on St. Pierre's Cathedral was finished in 1844 – it's the third cathedral on this site and, like many churches and castles built over several centuries, it reflects a variety of architectural styles and eras. In this case, its stoic, Gothic exterior gives way to a warm ambience of rich browns and golds on the inside.

Another dominating structure is the 18th century Town Hall (*Hôtel de Ville*) on the beautiful Place de la Mairie, a stunning public square that juts up against the Place du Palais – a perfect place to view the Parliamentary building of Brittany (*Palais du Parlement de Bretagne*).

🌍 Fougères & Vitré

Château de Fougères

Pl. Pierre-Simon

Tel: 02 99 99 79 59

www.chateau-fougeres.com

Château de Vitré

5 Rue Rallon

BRITTANY TRAVEL GUIDE

Tel: 02 99 75 04 54

Château des Rochers-Sévigné

Route d'Argentré-du-Plessis

Tel: 02 99 96 76 51

About 25 miles to the east of Rennes lies Fougères and Vitré, two small towns with stunning chateaux. Both towns have the distinction of being labeled "towns of art and history" by the French Ministry of Culture and Communication – an honor similar to being determined a UNESCO world heritage site.

Fougères' medieval castle was originally built by the Duchy of Brittany to keep the French out of their lands (which ultimately didn't work). With its impressive thirteen towers and beautiful belfry (one of only three in Brittany)

BRITTANY TRAVEL GUIDE

that serves as the centerpiece of a market on the weekends, this castle is one of the largest medieval fortresses still in existence.

Vitré is said to be one of the best-preserved medieval cities in Brittany. It is home to two prominent chateaux. The first (and foremost) is the Chateau de Vitré. This castle's pencil-point turrets call to mind fairytale settings.

The Chateau des Rochers-Sévigné is a (relatively) smaller gothic manor that was home to Mme de Sévigné, one of France's most celebrated letter writers and chronicler of the court of Louis XIV. Have a picnic on the grounds here, or play a round of golf on the manor's beautiful golf course.

 Josselin

Chateau de Josselin

Place de la Congrégation

Tel: 02 97 22 36 45

http://www.chateaujosselin.com/en/

Kerguéhennec Sculpture Garden

Bignan, Morbihan

Tel: 02 97 60 31 84

http://www.kerguehennec.fr/parc-de-sculptures

If you head west from Rennes you'll pass through Paimpont Forest. Be sure to get out of the car and spend some time in Paimpont Forest before you get to Josselin.

BRITTANY TRAVEL GUIDE

Paimpont is said to be the Brocéliande forest in the tales of Chrétien de Troyes.

If you aren't familiar with Chrétien or his forest, you've probably heard of his characters: King Arthur and Merlin, who is said to have met the Lady of the Lake in this forest (and is also said to be entombed here).

Josselin is a tiny village, but its medieval chateau on the river Oust is worth the visit. After exploring the grounds, check out the castle's doll museum, which showcases over 400 dolls from as many years.

The beautiful 12th century Basilica de Notre Dame du Roncier is another fine example of medieval architecture. A climb up the stairs to its bell tower provides stunning views of Josselin and the region.

You won't want to miss the Kerguéhennec sculpture garden located a short drive west of Josselin. Set on the grounds of Kerguéhennec, a stately white chateau built in 1710, the sculpture garden is one of very few in France. The works of over twenty major sculptors are on display year round here, and the chateau itself showcases temporary exhibitions of contemporary art.

 Dinan

Musée du Château (Castle Museum)

Château de la Duchesse Anne

Rue du Château

Tel: 02 96 39 45 20

BRITTANY TRAVEL GUIDE

Nestled along the hillsides of the Rance river valley that flows toward St-Malo and the sea sits Dinan, a modern yet medieval market town. It would be difficult to overpraise the beauty of this small city.

For a fantastic view of the entire city and the lay of the land, climb to the top of the 15th century d'Horloge Tower. Make your way back to the center by following any path you choose; the main sight to see in this town, perhaps more so than anywhere else, is the town itself, so plan to walk a lot.

Should rain drive you inside, check out Dinan's Castle Museum with its exhibition of local history. When the rain stops, continue walking outside the museum along the ramparts of the city wall and enjoy the splendor of this unique city.

 Saint-Malo

Château de St-Malo

Place Châteaubriand, near the marina

Tel: 02 99 40 71 57

Grand Aquarium

Rue de Général Patton

Tel: 02 99 21 19 00

http://www.aquarium-st-malo.com/

Situated on a fortified island, the city of Saint-Malo is a major attraction in Brittany. Its shoreline location may have something to do with its residents' fierce independence; it certainly has everything to do with the city's maritime history and dominance of the seas.

BRITTANY TRAVEL GUIDE

Saint-Malo was home to the corsairs – pirates commissioned by the crown – as well as true pirates. The city's sailors were some of the first Europeans to reach the New World. In fact, the Falkland Islands, known to the Argentinians as *Las Malvinas,* take their name from the French *Iles Malouines*.

There is much to see and do in Saint-Malo and it is one of the most visited places in Brittany. You can start in the Chateau de St-Malo, a 14th century castle that today houses a museum of the city's history, including artifacts from the age of the corsairs. Be sure to check out the view from its watchtowers. If you're looking for more maritime history, the Solidor Tower to the west of the city houses a nautical collection.

BRITTANY TRAVEL GUIDE

The place Vauban has a tropical aquarium built into its ramparts which you might want to check out, but don't get it confused with the Grand Aquarium on the edge of town. This aquarium – the second most visited tourist site in Brittany – brings some of the sea life to shore in a gigantic exhibition space. Among its 11,000 marine animals is an impressive shark tank.

During low tide, walk out to the Bé islands (carefully). On Petit Bé you'll find a dramatically situated fort built to in the 17th century to keep the British and Dutch away. On Grand Bé you'll find the tomb of Chateaubriand, the poet, diplomat, father of French Romanticism in literature and gourmet who gave his name to a delicious cut of steak. From the top of the Grand Bé you'll also enjoy beautiful views of the entire Emerald Coast.

While in St.-Malo you can visit the nearby town of **Cancale**. This photogenic fishing village is known as "the oyster capital" of Brittany. Cancale oysters were the preferred choice of Louis XIV; you can enjoy them in any number of restaurants, many of which offer seating with views of the bay looking outwards toward Mont St. Michel in the distance.

 Dinard

Casino Barriere de Dinard

4 Boulevard Wilson

Tel: 02 99 16 30 30

http://www.lucienbarriere.com/fr/Casino/Dinard/accueil.html

BRITTANY TRAVEL GUIDE

Dinard Golf Club

53 Boulevard de la Houle, Saint-Briac-sur-Mer

Tel: 02 99 88 32 07

http://www.dinardgolf.com/site/main.html

Continuing down the Emerald Coast, you'll come to Dinard. A seaside playground for British and American aristocrats in the Belle Époque of the late 19th century, Dinard of the 21st century is open to all but still has enough Victorian charm to be considered one of the most "British" seaside resorts in France (in fact, the town holds a Festival of British Cinema during the first week of October).

In keeping with its genteel pedigree, this is a beach town known for its sophistication, rather than a loud party atmosphere. Dinard has many excellent restaurants and bars, and if you're a gambler you'll definitely want to check out the Casino Barriere de Dinard, the largest casino in Brittany. Enjoy dinner there overlooking the town's biggest beach (Plage de l'Écluse), then try your luck at one of the slot machines.

The Dinard Golf Club is in the nearby town of Saint-Briac-sur-Mer. It is one of the oldest courses on continental Europe and is beautifully situated along the sea.

🌐 Pink Granite Coast (Côte du Granit Rose)

Glass Studios of Bréhat

Tel: 02 96 20 09 09

http://www.verreriesdebrehat.com/

BRITTANY TRAVEL GUIDE

Continuing along the coastline, you may notice that the rock formations have taken on a pinkish hue. This is due to the pink granite, which gives the coastline its name. This granite is quite rare and the only other places where it is found are in Corsica and China.

This part of the coast is especially popular with family vacationers. The scenery is breathtaking – pink cliffs against blue ocean water, and a temperate climate that allows for wildflowers at all parts of the year. There are many excellent walking trails for people of all ages; the walk between Trébeurden and Trégastel is particularly lovely.

Stop off in the port town of Tréguier, capital of the Tregor province. Its half-timbered architecture helps maintain much of its medieval market town character.

BRITTANY TRAVEL GUIDE

The city's cathedral is also a sight to behold: one of its three towers was funded by the Paris Lottery under Louis XVI and has windows in the shape of card suits! Have a bite to eat along the harbor overlooking the river Jaundy's many oyster beds.

Ile de Bréhat is only a short ferry ride away and the archipelago consists of two main islands (which are connected at low tide) and several smaller islands. The islands enjoy a warm gulf-stream microclimate and a lack of automobiles, making them a kind of oasis in a part of the country that you already thought couldn't be more relaxed.

The small town square offers several restaurants, bars and cafes with a variety of cuisines. Popular sights to see include the islands' lighthouses and the Verreries of Brehat. These glass studios located in the Citadel make exceptional glasswares, both functional and decorative.

 Morlaix & Roscoff

Queen Anne's House

33 rue du Mur

Tel: 02 98 88 23 26

http://www.mda-morlaix.com/

Château de Suscinio

Ploujean

Tel: 02 98 67 53 38

Continuing along the northern coast you'll come to Brittany's westernmost region, Finistière (from the Latin

BRITTANY TRAVEL GUIDE

Finis Terrae, literally, "End of the Earth"). Two of the first stops you'll want to make are the towns of Morlaix and Roscoff.

Morlaix is an old Breton port once infamous for its pirates (even more so than St-Malo). You won't find too many pirates today. Instead, the first thing you'll probably notice is the strikingly enormous viaduct towering above the city. Like the remains of the city wall and castle, the viaduct is built from the local pink granite, giving it a beautiful hue in the right light. The city's harbor and marina are particularly good places to view the viaduct and the unique beauty of Morlaix.

For a glimpse of the city's past, check out Queen Anne's House. Built in the 1600s, it's one of the oldest homes in the city and today houses a museum dedicated to the art

BRITTANY TRAVEL GUIDE

and artifacts of the 17th century. For history of the Finistière region, visit the Museum of the Jacobins.

If you stop for a drink, try a glass of Coreff, a locally brewed artisanal beer. After that, visit the Botanical Gardens at the Château de Suscinio. Situated on the grounds of the 1000-year-old castle, these gardens are the perfect place to wander and imagine medieval fairytales come to life.

Nearby Roscoff was labeled "Small Town of Character" by the French government in 2009. This is in part due to its quaint, seaside architecture and the granite mansions built by ship owners in the 16th and 17th centuries.

Britons of a certain age will remember a time when ubiquitous "Onion Johnnies" – Breton farmers dressed in

BRITTANY TRAVEL GUIDE

striped shirts and berets who sell braids of onions from their bikes by going door to door in Great Britain – crossed the English Channel from Roscoff to hawk their wares.

Although they began to decline in the 1950s, the Johnnies are making a comeback with the growth of the local agriculture movement and are still departing form Roscoff. The city celebrates the Johnnies at the Onion Johnny museum and holds an onion festival every summer.

Nestled in the Elorn Valley very close to Roscoff and Morlaix are several fine examples of Parish Closes. These are huge, ornate parish church complexes enclosed by a wall that in some ways look more like monasteries or abbeys.

They reflect both the spiritual fervor and the Celtic ancestry of the Bretons, as well as the general wealth enjoyed by the region in the 15th-18th centuries. Three parish closes that are particularly well maintained and beautiful are those of St.-Thégonnec, Guimliau, and Lampaul-Guimliau, but there are at least thirteen others to visit in the area.

 Brest

Oceanopolis

Port de Plaisance du Moulin Blanc

Tel: 02 98 34 40 40

http://www.oceanopolis.co.uk/

Ecomusée d'Ouessant

Maison du Niou, Ile d'Ouessant

BRITTANY TRAVEL GUIDE

Tel: 02 98 48 86

The city of Brest was almost completely destroyed during the WWII Battle of Brest. For this reason, it looks today much more of a modern city than others in Brittany. Brest's natural harbor has ensured its continued utilization as a commercial and military port for centuries.

To get a sense of what Brest looked like before the war, visit the museum in the 14th century Tanguy Tower. There you'll find expertly built dioramas of Brest through the ages. You'll also enjoy excellent views overlooking the river Penfield towards Brest's castle, which is also still in tact, and the impressive Recouvrance Bridge, the second largest vertical-lift bridge in Europe.

BRITTANY TRAVEL GUIDE

One of Brest's top attractions is Oceanopolis, a wildly futuristic-looking building that houses four aquarium pavilions, three of which are dedicated to a different maritime zone (tropical, polar, temperate) and one (a rotating exhibition pavilion) dedicated to celebrating biodiversity.

Just south and east of Brest you'll find the Armorican Regional Nature Park, a vast preserve that covers 1,250 km^2, stretching from the moors of Monts d'Arrée to the Ile d'Ouessant.

The park's natural diversity presents visitors with views of the stark, rolling hillsides of the moors, mountains that are older than the alps, and islands that have been labeled by UNESCO as biosphere reserves for their populations of

BRITTANY TRAVEL GUIDE

sea birds, otters and beavers (among many other animals).

Dotting the landscape you'll also find evidence of the people that have lived there through the ages, whether through Celtic and early Christian chapels and sites of worship, or even older monuments from prehistoric times.

The Ile d'Ouessant is the westernmost point of metropolitan France. A visit to the island provides you with breathtaking and windswept ocean views that might even include a peek at the local seal population. The Ecomusée d'Ouessant sells unique furniture made from driftwood and wrecks.

🌍 Douarnenez & Locronan

Continuing down the western coast, you'll come to Douarnenez, a small city with several interesting quirks. Douarnenez used to be the sardine capital of France, and although the sardine business has slowed in recent years, a great way to see the city is to follow the Sardine Route. This is a walk that follows nineteen different panels explaining the history of the city and the sardine fishing industry along the way.

A wealth of legend surrounds Douarnenez. It figures prominently in the Tristan and Iseult story – and at low tide you can walk to Tristan Island which today is a nature preserve. It is also believed to be the site of the City of Ys, an imaginary city that, like Atlantis, sunk beneath the ocean waters at some point.

BRITTANY TRAVEL GUIDE

Legend has it that Ys was ruled by a lusty queen who had nightly orgies and killed her lovers in the morning. The city was punished for her sins and ended up getting swallowed by the Douarnenez Bay where it has since been buried and forgotten.

Every year there are festivals to celebrate the area's rich folklore, fishing industry and nautical traditions. You can enjoy these after spending your morning sunbathing on one of several beaches or walking along the Port Rhu where the yachts and fishing boats are moored.

A few kilometers away you'll find Locronan, a well-preserved historic Breton village. The town is certified as one of "The Most Beautiful Villages of France" – an actual designation awarded to 152 villages in France (and one of six in Brittany) that meet certain criteria.

Locronan is known, in addition to its beauty, for an important pilgrimage route that ends in its church dedicated to St. Ronan, a Celtic saint who is strongly venerated throughout Brittany.

🌎 Quimper

When Celts from Cornwall, UK settled in Brittany, they gave their new home the same name as the old, only the French spell it a little differently: Cornuaille. Quimper was the capital of ancient Cornuaille, and although the region no longer exists as such, Quimper is still the unofficial capital of Celtic Brittany.

A walk through Old Quimper will make this apparent, as the sounds of Breton music fill the streets from the open

BRITTANY TRAVEL GUIDE

shop doors where traditional Breton clothing and crafts are on display in the windows.

In Old Quimper you'll see the city's cathedral. Dedicated to St. Corentin, one of the founder saints of Brittany, the cathedral is unusual for a Gothic church in that its form bends in the middle, rather than maintaining a strict cruciform. This was to avoid building on top of a swamp.

To the west of the cathedral you'll see the rustic charm of the old quarter's half-timbered shops. Here you should sample the local crepes, said to be the best in Brittany.

Quimper's art museum has a wonderful collection of works from the 14th century to the present, but is particularly strong in exhibiting painters whose works

BRITTANY TRAVEL GUIDE

depict a romantic view of Brittany, including many of the Pont-Aven school.

If you're in Quimper during the end of July you have the opportunity to attend the Cornwall Festival, a cultural celebration that lasts for six days. Over 200 performances of local music and dance are scheduled around town, many of which are free.

Down the road from Quimper is **Concarneau**, a small port town whose main attraction is the Ville Close – a perfectly preserved walled city located on an island in the harbor. The Ville Close was a center of shipbuilding, but today tourism is its main industry and it boasts many restaurants and cafes in an incredibly charming atmosphere.

🌍 Auray, Carnac & Quiberon

Another quaint port town, you'll want to see the several beautiful churches in Auray and stroll along its atmospheric streets. Use Auray as your base from which to explore Carnac and the island of Quiberon.

Carnac is a must-see. The town is famous for its more than 10,000 *menhirs*, standing stones erected by the pre-Celtic Neolithic people of lower Brittany. This is the largest collection of Neolithic stone monuments anywhere in the world and it is believed to have been there since 3300 BC.

The western shore of the Quiberon peninsula is known as "The Wild Coast" with its cliffs and rock formations that have been beaten by wind and rain. You'll enjoy the drive along here on your way to the town of Quiberon. In town, take a carriage ride, visit one of the local spas (you can certainly use a massage after all the walking and hiking you've been doing!), and enjoy some excellently prepared seafood.

🌐 Vannes

Vannes is situated along the Gulf of Morbihan, a modern commercial city with a well-preserved past. Enjoy a walk along the city's well-landscaped medieval wall and take in Vannes from many different angles. In the Place des Lices let your mind wander back 800 years and imagine the jousts that used to take place here.

At the time of the jousts, *la Cohue* was a covered medieval market and forum, but today is a museum of fine art. The 15th century Château Gaillard houses the history museum with a fine collection of prehistoric artifacts.

BRITTANY TRAVEL GUIDE

Enjoy lunch along the harbor and then take a boat ride around the gulf. You can pick up a boat tour in the Parc du Golfe about a mile south from the town center.

Budget Tips

 Accommodation

Rennes

Mercure Rennes Centre Parlement

1 rue Paul Louis Courtier

Tel: 02 99 78 82 20

http://www.accorhotels.com/gb/hotel-1056-mercure-rennes-centre-parlement/index.shtml

The Mercure is quietly nestled into a side street in the city center, a quick walk away from the metro station and train station. The bustle of the pedestrian streets with their cafes, restaurants, bars and shops are also very close.

Rooms start at €85.00 and include 24 hour reception, a bar, garage, room service, free WiFi, satellite television, air conditioning and hair dryer.

St. Malo

Le Nautilus

9, rue de la Corne de Cerf

Tel: 02 99 40 42 27

http://www.lenautilus.com/

This highly recommended hotel is known for its great location, friendly staff and bright, clean rooms. Rooms are not huge, but they are great for the price (a double room ranges from €62-70 depending on the time of year you're traveling). The Nautilus has a bar and breakfast available for an extra fee.

Rooms are all non-smoking and come equipped with WiFi connection, LCD televisions with channels in French and English.

Brest

Hotel Abalys
7 Avenue Georges Clemenceau
Tel: 02 98 44 21 86
http://www.abalys.com/en

The Hotel Abalys sits in the heart of Brest across from the Palais de Congrés and the Le Quartz theatre. From here you'll be just minutes away from Siam and Jaurès streets (for shopping) as well as the Tanguy Tower and castle. Rooms either overlook the sea or a lovely park, so a great view in any case.

All rooms come equipped with free WiFi, 24-hour reception, and complimentary continental breakfast. There is a bar in the hotel and parking (for €4/day), and if you book through the website you can arrange for free bicycles. Rates range from €45-79.

Quimper

Hotel Escale Oceania
6 rue Theodore le Hars
Tel: 02 98 53 37 37
http://www.oceaniahotels.com/hotel-escale-oceania-quimper?lg=UK

This hotel has an excellent location looking across the river at Old Quimper and the cathedral. The hotel has just completed a six-month renovation process at the time of this writing, so it 64 rooms – which were already clean and spacious – now have new parquet flooring and modern furniture.

The bathrooms are now equipped with Italian style showers, large mirrors (and hair dryers so you can travel light). The staff is known to be attentive and accommodating. Prices start at €55.

Rooms are air-conditioned, there is free WiFi, meeting rooms and a business office with internet access and printing. Room service is available.

Vannes

Kyriad Vannes Centre

8 Place de la Liberation

Tel: 02 97 63 27 36

http://www.kyriad-vannes.fr/UK/

Just a short walk away from Vannes' medieval city center, you'll enjoy being right in the midst of the rampart walls, the cathedral and the shops.

The building itself is historical, having served for many years as a post house. The hotel's restaurant – A l'Image Sainte-Anne – presents a menu of traditional Breton cuisine, both from the sea and the countryside.

Rooms include free WiFi, flat-screen televisions and air conditioning. Bathrooms are spacious and include a hair dryer. A free printing service is available in the lobby. Prices range from €54-69.

🌐 Restaurants, Cafés & Bars

Dinard

Bistro Resto Oliver

25 Boulevard Feart

Tel: 02 99 16 07 95

http://www.bistro-resto-oliver.fr/

This excellent bistro sits a short walk away from the water and offers a delicious menu of creative twists on regional Breton cuisine. Chef Oliver's creations include a veal cheeseburger topped with foie gras and seared foie gras with tagliatelle and a creamy morel mushroom sauce.

The chef himself will speak with you directly and make suggestions for wine pairings. You'll want to make reservations ahead of time as the restaurant is small and intimate; the ambience, unsurprisingly, is cozy and warm.

Prices range from $26-$52.

Vitré

Auberge Saint Louis

31, rue Notre Dame

Tel: 02 99 75 28 28

http://www.aubergesaintlouis.fr/

The Auberge Saint Louis offers a fixed price menu with extensive options, all of which is traditional French cuisine cooked and prepared at a high standard at a very reasonable price (most options are available a la carte as well).

The elegant wood paneled interior and artwork will take you back in time to the 17th century and only accentuate the old world charm of Vitré.

Auray

L'Eglantine

17 Place Saint Sauveur

Tel: 02 97 56 46 55

You don't come to L'Eglantine for the food – even though it's fantastic – you come for the décor and the experience. Walking through the doors you'll feel like Alice in Wonderland – assuming that when she walked through the rabbit hole she entered a phantasmagorically kitschy drag queen's lair!

Baubles, bangles and beads adorn every nook and cranny, along with pin-up posters and pink ostrich feathers galore. If it's kitschy, it's here. Madame Proprietor is the only thing serious around here, a somewhat stern presence amidst so much fun, but she is welcoming and attentive. The menu is predominantly seafood and well priced.

Quiberon

La Criee

11 Quai Ocean

Tel: 02 97 30 53 09

http://www.maisonlucas.net/restaurant.html

La Criee is a highly recommended seafood restaurant that sits right on harbor. The Lucas family who runs the restaurant (and shop) also runs the fishing boats (*and* they smoke the fish themselves!), so they will personally guarantee the freshness of your dish. Price range is $27-$34.

Douarnenez

Au Goûter breton chez Tudal

36 rue Jean Jaurès

Tel: 02 98 92 02 74

http://www.augouterbreton.com/

Brittany (and France in general) is not lacking for creperies, so of course they range greatly in quality and price. Seeing where the locals eat is a good way to figure out what's good and what isn't.

By using that standard of measurement, Au Gôuter breton must surely be one of the best. Don't plan on a quick bite;

Breton crepes are savory and filling – and at Au Gôuter breton you'll want to take your time with every bite. If you want to order like a local, as for your crepe "complete": filled with ham and cheese – and a fried egg for good measure.

 Shopping

Quimper

HB Henriot Boutique

Rue Haute, Locmaria

Tel: 02 98 9 09 36

http://www.henriot-quimper.com/en/actualite/index.php.html

If you're looking to take something home that is uniquely breton but not a kitschy souvenir, you should consider buying a few pieces of Quimper faïence. This kind of tin-glazed pottery originated in Italy but the process spread through Europe.

HB Henriot has been producing faïence since the reign of Louis XIV (in fact, it's one of the oldest continuously running businesses in France!), and then as now all their pieces are hand painted.

Whether you opt for decorative platters with images of Breton children in traditional garb, coffee mugs with pastoral scenes or a set of flatware with simple geometric images, your purchase will be a great conversation starter and a frequent reminder of your trip.

Roscoff

Roscoff's Wine Seller

Rue Great Torrington

Tel: 02 98 61 24 10

Brittany's boundaries no longer include the Loire Valley as they did centuries ago so Brittany isn't one of France's known wine regions. But that's no reason for you to go home without a few high quality bottles at low prices. You can find these at Roscoff's Wine Seller. In fact you'll probably want to pick up a few to enjoy on the beach as well as to take home.

Rennes

Cap Malo

Along the highway RN 137

The Cap Malo shopping center is just 10km from the Rennes city center. This American-style shopping center may not be the place for you if you've come to Brittany for old world charm, nevertheless it provides you with many shopping options in one easy location.

Cap Malo has eighteen boutiques that sell all kinds of clothing and furniture, as well as a handful of larger chain department stores, a movie theater, a 9-hole golf course, and a bowling alley with twenty-four lanes. Its food court has a number of fast-food options. It's on the road from Rennes to St-Malo.

Cancale

Grain de Vanille

12 place de la Victoire

Tel: 02 23 15 12 70

Les Entrepots Épices-Roellinger

1 Rue Duguesclin

BRITTANY TRAVEL GUIDE

Tel: 02 23 15 13 91

Foodies will want to try to recreate the scents of flavors of Brittany in their own kitchens. Cancale has several shops to help you along in this endeavor. At the Grain de Vanille you'll find many of the delights of Breton confectionery: salty butter caramels, ices and sorbets, uniquely flavored honeys.

Les Entrepots Épices-Roellinger sells spices from around the world, many of which Monsieur Roellinger has mixed into his personal blends – including Poudre du Vent, a blend of rare peppers, *fleur de sel* and vanilla perfect for cream sauces.

BRITTANY TRAVEL GUIDE

Know Before You Go

Entry Requirements

By virtue of the Schengen agreement, visitors from other countries in the European Union will not need a visa when visiting France. Additionally Swiss visitors are also exempt. Visitors from certain other countries such as Andorra, Canada, the United Kingdom, Ireland, the Bahamas, Australia, the USA, Chile, Costa Rica, Croatia, El Salvador, Guatemala, Honduras, Israel, Malaysia, Mauritius, Monaco, Nicaragua, New Zealand, Panama, Paraguay, Saint Kitts and Nevis, San Marino, the Holy See, Seychelles, Taiwan and Japan do not need visas for a stay of less than 90 days. Visitors to France must be in possession of a valid passport that expires no sooner than three months after the intended stay. UK citizens will not need a visa to enter France. Visitors must provide proof of residence, financial support and the reason for their visit. If you wish to work or study in France, however, you will need a visa.

🌐 Health Insurance

Citizens of other EU countries are covered for emergency health care in France. UK residents, as well as visitors from Switzerland are covered by the European Health Insurance Card (EHIC), which can be applied for free of charge. Visitors from non-Schengen countries will need to show proof of private health insurance that is valid for the duration of their stay in France (that offers at least €37,500 coverage), as part of their visa application. A letter of coverage will need to be submitted to the French Embassy along with your visa application. American travellers will need to check whether their regular medical insurance covers international travel. No special vaccinations are required.

🌐 Travelling with Pets

France participates in the Pet Travel Scheme (PETS) which allows UK residents to travel with their pets without requiring quarantine upon re-entry. Certain conditions will need to be met. The animal will have to be microchipped and up to date on rabies vaccinations. In the case of dogs, France also requires vaccination against distemper. If travelling from another EU member country, you will need an EU pet passport. Regardless of the country, a Declaration of Non-Commercial Transport must be signed stating that you do not intend to sell your pet.

A popular form of travel with pets between the UK and France is via the Eurotunnel, which has special facilities for owners travelling with pets. This includes dedicated pet exercise areas and complimentary dog waste bags. Transport of a pet via this medium costs €24. The Calais Terminal has a special Pet Reception Building. Pets travelling from the USA will need to be at least 12 weeks old and up to date on rabies vaccinations. Microchipping or some form of identification tattoo will also be required. If travelling from another country, do inquire about the specific entry requirements for your pet into France and also about re-entry requirements in your own country.

Airports

There are three airports near Paris where most international visitors arrive. The largest of these is **Charles De Gaulle** (CDG) airport, which serves as an important hub for both international and domestic carriers. It is located about 30km outside Paris and is well-connected to the city's rail network. Most trans-Atlantic flights arrive here. **Orly** (ORY) is the second largest and oldest airport serving Paris. It is located 18km south of the city and is connected to several public transport options including a bus service, shuttle service and Metro rail. Most of its arrivals and departures are to other destinations within Europe. **Aéroport de Paris-Beauvais-Tillé** (BVA), which lies in Tillé near Beauvais, about 80km outside

BRITTANY TRAVEL GUIDE

Paris, is primarily used by Ryanair for its flights connecting Paris to Dublin, Shannon Glasgow and other cities.

There are several important regional airports. **Aéroport Nice Côte d'Azur** (NCE) is the 3rd busiest airport in France and serves as a gateway to the popular French Riviera. **Aéroport Lyon Saint-Exupéry** (LYS) lies 20km east of Lyon and serves as the main hub for connections to the French Alps and Provence. It is the 4th busiest airport of France. **Aéroport de Bordeaux** (BOD) served the region of Bordeaux. **Aéroport de Toulouse – Blagnac** (TLS), which lies 7km from Toulouse, provides access to the south-western part of France. **Aéroport de Strasbourg** (SXB), which lies 10km west of Strasbourg, served as a connection to Orly, Paris and Nice. **Aéroport de Marseille Provence** (MRS) is located in the town of Marignane, about 27km from Marseille and provides access to Provence and the French Riviera. **Aéroport Nantes Atlantique** (NTE) lies in Bouguenais, 8km from Nantes carriers and provides a gateway to the regions of Normandy and Brittany in the western part of France. **Aéroport de Lille** (LIL) is located near Lesquin and provides connections to the northern part of France.

🌐 Airlines

Air France is the national flag carrier of France and in 2003, it merged with KLM. The airline has a Flying Blue rewards

BRITTANY TRAVEL GUIDE

program, which allows members to earn, accumulate and redeem Flying Blue Miles on any flights with Air France, KLM or any other Sky Team airline. This includes Aeroflot, Aerolineas Argentinas, AeroMexico, Air Europa, Alitalia, China Airlines, China Eastern, China Southern, Czech Airlines, Delta, Garuda Indonesia, Kenya Airways, Korean Air, Middle Eastern Airlines, Saudia, Tarom, Vietnam Airlines and Xiamen Airlines.

Air France operates several subsidiaries, including the low-cost Transavia.com France, Cityjet and Hop! It is also in partnership with Air Corsica. Other French airlines are Corsairfly and XL Airways France (formerly Star Airlines).

France's largest intercontinental airport, Charles de Gaulle serves as a hub for Air France, as well as its regional subsidiary, HOP!. It also functions as a European hub for Delta Airlines. Orly Airport, also in Paris, serves as the main hub for Air France's low cost subsidiary, Transavia, with 40 different destinations, including London, Madrid, Copenhagen, Moscow, Casablanca, Algiers, Amsterdam, Istanbul, Venice, Rome, Berlin and Athens. Aéroport de Marseille Provence (MRS) outside Marseille serves as a hub to the region for budget airlines such as EasyJet and Ryanair. Aéroport Nantes Atlantique serves as a French base for the Spanish budget airline, Volotea.

BRITTANY TRAVEL GUIDE

🌐 Currency

France's currency is the Euro. It is issued in notes in denominations of €500, €200, €100, €50, €20, €10 and €5. Coins are issued in €2, €1, 50c, 20c, 10c, 5c, 2c and 1c.

🌐 Banking & ATMs

If your ATM card is compatible with the MasterCard/Cirrus or Visa/Plus networks and configured for a 4-digit PIN, you will have no problem drawing money in France. Most French ATMs have an English language option. Remember to inform your bank of your travel plans before you leave. Keep an eye open around French ATMs to avoid pickpockets or scammers.

🌐 Credit Cards

Credit cards are frequently used throughout France, not just in shops, but also to pay for metro tickets, parking tickets, and motorway tolls and even to make phone calls at phone booths. MasterCard and Visa are accepted by most vendors. American Express and Diners Club are also accepted by the more tourist oriented businesses. Credit cards issued in Europe are smart cards that that are fitted with a microchip and require a PIN for each transaction. This means that a few ticket machines, self-service vendors and other businesses may not be configured to accept the older magnetic strip credit cards.

🌐 Tourist Taxes

All visitors to France pay a compulsory city tax or tourist tax ("taxe de séjour"), which is payable at your accommodation. Children are exempt from tourist tax. The rate depends on the standard of accommodation, starting with €0.75 per night for cheaper establishments going up to €4, for the priciest options. Rates are, of course, subject to change.

🌐 Reclaiming VAT

If you are not from the European Union, you can claim back VAT (or Value Added Tax) paid on your purchases in France. The VAT rate in France is 20 percent on most goods, but restaurant goods, food, transport and medicine are charged at lower rates. VAT can be claimed back on purchases of over €175 from the same shop, provided that your stay in France does not exceed six months. Look for shops that display a "Tax Free" sign. The shop assistant must fill out a form for reclaiming VAT. When you submit it at the airport, you can expect your refund to be debited within 30 to 90 days to your credit card or bank account. It can also be sent by cheque.

🌎 Tipping Policy

In French restaurants, a 15 percent service charge is added directly to your bill and itemized with the words *service compris* or "tip included". This is a legal requirement for taxation purposes. If the service was unusually good, a little extra will be appreciated. In an expensive restaurant where there is a coat check, you may add €1 per coat. In a few other situations, a tip will be appreciated. You can give an usherette in a theatre 50 cents to €1, give a porter €1 per bag for helping with your luggage or show your appreciation for a taxi driver with 5-10 percent over the fare. It is also customary to tip a hair dresser or a tour guide 10 percent.

🌎 Mobile Phones

Most EU countries, including France uses the GSM mobile service. This means that most UK phones and some US and Canadian phones and mobile devices will work in France. While you could check with your service provider about coverage before you leave, using your own service in roaming mode will involve additional costs. The alternative is to purchase a French SIM card to use during your stay in France. France has four mobile networks. They are Orange, SFR, Bouygues Telecom and Free. In France, foreigners are barred from applying for regular phone contract and the data rates are somewhat pricier on pre-paid phone services than in most European countries. You will need to show some form of identification, such as a passport when you make your purchase and it can take up to 48 hours to activate a French SIM card. If there is an Orange Boutique nearby, you can buy a SIM for €3.90. Otherwise, the Orange Holiday package is available for €39.99. Orange also sells a 4G device which enables your own portable Wi-Fi hotspot for €54.90. SFR offers a SIM card, simply known as le card for €9.99. Data rates begin at €5 for 20Mb.

Dialling Code

The international dialling code for France is +33.

Emergency Numbers

All emergencies: (by mobile) 112
Police: 17
Medical Assistance: 15
Fire and Accidents: 18
SOS All Emergencies (hearing assisted: 114)
Visa: 0800 90 11 79
MasterCard: 0800 90 13 87
American Express: 0800 83 28 20

Public Holidays

1 January: New Year's Day (Nouvel an / Jour de l'an / Premier de l'an)

BRITTANY TRAVEL GUIDE

March - April: Easter Monday (Lundi de Pâques)

1 May: Labor Day (Fête du Travail / Fête des Travailleurs)

8 May: Victory in Europe Day (Fête de la Victoire)

May: Ascension Day (Ascension)

May: Whit Monday (Lundi de Pentecôte)

14 July: Bastille Day (Fête nationale)

15 August: Assumption of Mary (L'Assomption de Marie)

1 November: All Saints Day (La Toussaint)

11 November: Armistace Day (Armistice de 1918)

25 December: Christmas Day (Noël)

Good Friday and St Stephens Day (26 December) are observed only in Alsace and Moselle.

🌎 Time Zone

France falls in the Central European Time Zone. This can be calculated as Greenwich Mean Time/Co-ordinated Universal Time (GMT/UTC) +2; Eastern Standard Time (North America) -6; Pacific Standard Time (North America) -9.

🌎 Daylight Savings Time

Clocks are set forward one hour on the last Sunday of March and set back one hour on the last Sunday of October for Daylight Savings Time.

🌍 School Holidays

The academic year in France is from the beginning of September to the end of June. The long summer holiday is from the beginning of July to the end of August. There are three shorter vacation periods. All schools break up for a two week break around Christmas and New Year. There are also two week breaks in February and April, but this varies per region, as French schools are divided into three zones, which take their winter and spring vacations at different times.

🌍 Driving Laws

The French drive on the ride hand side of the road. If you have a non-European driving licence, you will be able to use it in France, provided that the licence is valid and was issued in your country of residence before the date of your visa application. There are a few other provisions. The minimum driving age in France is 18. Your licence will need to be in French or alternately, you must carry a French translation of your driving permit with you.

In France, the speed limit depends on weather conditions. In dry weather, the speed limit is 130km per hour for highways, 110km per hour for 4-lane expressways and 90km per hour for 2 or 3-lane rural roads. In rainy weather, this is reduced to 110km, 100km and 80km per hour respectively. In foggy weather with poor visibility, the speed limit is 50km per hour on all roads. On urban roads, the speed limit is also 50km per hour.

By law, French drivers are obliged to carry a breathalyser in their vehicle, but these are available from most supermarkets, chemists and garages for €1. The legal limit is 0.05, but for new drivers who have had their licence for less than three years, it is 0.02. French motorways are called autorouts. It is illegal in France to use a mobile phone while driving, even if you have a headset.

Drinking Laws

The legal drinking age in France is 18. The drinking policy regarding public spaces will seem confusing to outsiders. Each municipal area imposes its own laws. In Paris, alcohol consumption is only permitted in licensed establishments. It is strictly forbidden in parks and public gardens.

Smoking Laws

From 2007, smoking has been banned in indoor spaces such as schools, government buildings, airports, offices and factories in France. The ban was extended in 2008 to hospitality venues such as restaurants, bars, cafes and casinos. French trains have been smoke free since December 2004.

BRITTANY TRAVEL GUIDE

🌐 Electricity

Electricity: 220-240 volts

Frequency: 50 Hz

Electricity sockets in France are unlike those of any other country. They are hermaphroditic, meaning that they come equipped with both prongs and indents. When visiting from the UK, Ireland, the USA or even another European country, you will need a special type of adaptor to accommodate this. If travelling from the USA, you will also need a converter or step-down transformer to convert the current to to 110 volts, to avoid damage to your appliances. The latest models of many laptops, camcorders, mobile phones and digital cameras are dual-voltage with a built in converter.

🌐 Food & Drink

France is a paradise for dedicated food lovers and the country has a vast variety of well-known signature dishes. These include foie gras, bouillabaisse, escargots de Bourgogne, Coq au vin, Bœuf Bourguignon, quiche Lorraine and ratatouille. A great budget option is crêpes or pancakes. Favorite sweets and pastries include éclairs, macarons, mille-feuilles, crème brûlée and croissants.

The country is home to several world-famous wine-growing regions, including Alsace, Bordeaux, Bourgogne, Champagne,

BRITTANY TRAVEL GUIDE

Corse, Côtes du Rhône, Languedoc-Roussillon, Loire, Provence and Sud-Ouest and correctly matching food to complimentary wine choices is practically a science. Therein lies the key to enjoying wine as the French do. It accompanies the meal. Drinking wine when it is not lunch or dinner time is sure to mark you as a foreigner. Pastis and dry vermouth are popular aperitifs and favorite after-dinner digestifs include cognac, Armagnac, calvados and eaux de vie. The most popular French beer is Kronenbourg, which originates from a brewery that dates back to 1664.

Websites

http://www.rendezvousenfrance.com/
http://www.france.com/
http://www.francethisway.com/
http://www.france-voyage.com/en/
http://www.francewanderer.com/
http://wikitravel.org/en/France
http://www.bonjourlafrance.com/index.aspx

Printed in Great Britain
by Amazon